INVESTIGATE EARTH SCIENCE

Barbara Allman

GLACIERS

E **Enslow Publishing**
101 W. 23rd Street
Suite 240
New York, NY 10011
USA
enslow.com

•• Words to Know

basin A dip in the earth that is shaped like a bowl.

calving A large piece of glacier ice breaking off and falling into the ocean.

continent One of the earth's seven large areas of land.

crevasse A deep crack in a glacier.

debris Pieces that are left behind when something is destroyed.

iceberg A huge chunk of ice floating in the ocean with only a small part above water.

moraine A collection of rocks and earth that are left by a glacier as it moves.

valley A long, low place on the earth's surface. It is made by a glacier or river.

Contents

Frozen Giant

● ● ● A glacier is a large area of thick ice. This frozen giant is on the move! Some people call glaciers "rivers of ice." They flow very slowly over land. A glacier is so slow that you might not even be able to see it move.

Where Glaciers Are Found

Every **continent** but Australia has glaciers. Glaciers are found at the tops of snowy mountains. They are also found at the North and South Poles. Most glaciers are in Greenland and Antarctica. These are huge, spreading ice sheets.

A glacier slowly flows down a valley.

These mountains have ice caps at the top. These are a kind of glacier.

Locked in Ice

Living things need fresh water. Only a tiny part of the earth's water is fresh water. Most of our planet's fresh water is frozen in glaciers.

Types of Glaciers

An ice cap is one kind of glacier. You can see an ice cap at the top of a mountain. It looks white and snowy. Other mountain glaciers flow down wide places between mountains. The wide places are **valleys**. An ice sheet is another kind of glacier. It is spread out. Huge ice sheets cover Antarctica for hundreds of miles.

How Glaciers Form

It may take thousands of years for a glacier to form. Glaciers form when snow falls in a place that is always cold. Here is how it happens: Snow falls near a mountaintop and does not melt away. More and more snow falls. Each layer of snow presses down. This makes the snow at the bottom become ice. The ice gets thicker with every snowfall. Then the ice starts to flow. It is now a glacier.

How Glaciers Move

The great weight of glaciers causes them to move. Glaciers move by sliding on a thin layer of water. The water is from melted ice. Some glaciers also creep. This is when some layers move forward faster than others. The top and middle move faster than the bottom and sides.

This date marker shows how much the glacier has moved back because of melting.

The glacier was here in
Le glacier était ici en

1908

Glaciers pull back or push forward. A glacier may pull back if it starts to melt. It may push forward if there is more snowfall. This happens very slowly.

When Glaciers Break Up

Glacier ice is hard, but it can break. When glaciers move, the ice may crack. The cracks in a glacier are called **crevasses**. Scientists who study glaciers must watch for danger. Crevasses can be wide and deep.

Deadly Iceberg

The *Titanic* was the largest ocean liner of its time. People said it could not sink, but it did. On its first trip, it struck an iceberg. Many lives were lost when the *Titanic* sank.

The scientist at the top is exploring a glacier with a deep crevasse.

Part of this glacier is falling into the sea. This is known as calving.

Glaciers at the edges of the oceans crack, too. A piece of a giant glacier breaks off. Splash! It falls into the ocean with a loud roar. This is called **calving**. Calving produces floating **icebergs**. Icebergs are a danger to ships. The largest part of an iceberg lies under the water. Only a small part shows. Passing ships cannot see the large part. A ship can strike an iceberg and sink.

Shaping the Land

You may live in a place that once was covered by a glacier. The last ice age ended around eleven thousand years ago. What was the ice age like? One-third of the earth was covered by glaciers. Ice age glaciers changed the land.

Parts of Lake Michigan freeze over in winter. Like all of the Great Lakes, it was created by glaciers over thousands of years.

Basins

Glaciers scrape the land and carry it away. They push aside broken rocks and soil. They wear down sides of mountains. Glaciers also cut deep **basins** in the earth. A basin is like a huge bowl. The basins fill with water and make new lakes and rivers.

Lake Makers

Glaciers made the five Great Lakes of North America. Lake Superior is the biggest one. It has a larger surface than any other lake in the world.

Moraines

A glacier travels downhill. It scrapes the soil below it. It wears down the sides of a mountain. It carries the **debris** along. Rocks and soil pile up at the edges of the glacier's path. The mounds of rock left by a glacier are **moraines**.

The glaciers of the last ice age melted. They left their mark. Mountains were worn down. There were new valleys and hills. There were new lakes, rivers, and streams. Glaciers had shaped the land.

The soil and rocks are moved by the glacier and pile up along its edges, forming moraines.

15

Our Changing Earth

Ice ages have happened for millions of years. In between them, the earth has become warmer. Scientists study glaciers to find out more about this. They ask questions. When did the earth warm up? When did ice ages happen?

Drilling into the Ice

Scientists drill into Antarctic ice. They fill tubes with the ice. Bubbles in the ice tell a story. What was the air like long ago? Maybe there were lots of plants producing oxygen. Maybe a volcano sent ash into the air. Maybe there was smoke from forest fires. Many things in the ice can tell scientists what happened long ago.

This scientist is working on a glacial ice sheet in Greenland. He is studying the effects of global warming on the ice.

Scientists drill into the ice to get a core sample. They can tell a lot from what the different layers of ice show.

Disappearing Glaciers

Glaciers are melting. Earth's temperatures are getting warmer. Scientists say some glaciers have disappeared. More are disappearing right now. Planes and satellites take pictures from above. People are watching the glaciers change. If enough glaciers melted, would sea levels rise? Would there be flooding along the coasts? Scientists want to know.

Melting Away

The glaciers in Montana's Glacier National Park are melting. They are thousands of years old. But they may be gone by 2030.

The Earth Is Warming

The last hundred years have been the warmest in four thousand years. Will the earth continue to get warmer? Scientists are studying the question. They say that people add to the warming. People burn dirty fuels that make the earth warmer. Glaciers around the world are shrinking.

Scientists will always study ways to help our planet. What will our planet be like in another hundred years? One thing is certain. The earth is always changing.

The pool of water seen here comes from melting glaciers. Global warming is causing glaciers around the world to shrink.

Activity: Build a Glacier Model

●●○ You will need:
- sand
- gravel
- water
- ice cubes
- small plastic dish
- your freezer

Glaciers have layers of snow. They also pick up rocks and soil. Make a model to show the layers of a glacier.

Step 1: Place ice cubes in the dish. Pour water over them. Leave space at the top. Freeze overnight.

Step 2: Take out the frozen dish. Add a little sand and gravel on top of the ice. Pour a centimeter of water over it. Freeze. Do this as many times as you like.

Step 3: Remove the frozen glacier from the dish. Draw a picture of your glacier model.

Can you see layers? Are they all the same? Do the older ice and newer ice look the same?

What could you do next with your glacier model?

Glaciers are made up of many layers of snow, soil, and rocks.

Learn More

Books

Higgins, Nadia. *Welcome to Glacier National Park*. Mankato, MN: The Child's World, 2018.

Prokos, Anna, and Jamie Tablason. *Ice Queen: Exploring Icebergs and Glaciers*. Minneapolis, MN: Red Chair Press, 2017.

Simon, Seymour. *Icebergs and Glaciers*. New York, NY: HarperCollins, 2018.

Websites

Denali
www.nps.gov/dena/learn/nature/upload/Glaciers_Kids_2014.pdf
View maps and pictures of glaciers in Denali National Park.

Glacier National Park Webcams
www.nps.gov/glac/learn/photosmultimedia/webcams.htm
Enjoy live views of different places in Glacier National Park.

OneGeology Kids
www.onegeology.org/extra/kids/earthprocesses/glaciers.html
Check out glacier photos with simple text about earth processes.

Index

Published in 2020 by Enslow Publishing, LLC.
101 W. 23rd Street, Suite 240, New York, NY 10011

Library of Congress Cataloging-in-Publication Data
Names: Allman, Barbara, author.
Title: Glaciers / Barbara Allman.
Description: New York : Enslow Publishing, 2020. | Series: Investigate earth science | Includes bibliographical references and index. | Audience: Grades K-4.
Identifiers: LCCN 2018047002| ISBN 9781978507418 (library bound) | ISBN 9781978508620 (pbk.) | ISBN 9781978508637 (6 pack)
Subjects: LCSH: Glaciers—Juvenile literature.
Classification: LCC GB2403.8 .A47 2020 | DDC 551.31/2—dc23
LC record available at https://lccn.loc.gov/2018047002

Printed in the United States of America

To Our Readers: We have done our best to make sure all website addresses in this book were active and appropriate when we went to press. However, the author and the publisher have no control over and assume no liability for the material available on those websites or on any websites they may link to. Any comments or suggestions can be sent by e-mail to customerservice@enslow.com.

Photos Credits: Cover, p. 1 Christopher Wood/Shutterstock.com; pp. 3, 5 Tupungato/Shutterstock.com; pp. 3, 6 kavram/Shutterstock.com; pp. 3, 13 WillWight/Shutterstock.com; pp. 3, 15 Autumn Sky Photography/Shutterstock .com; pp. 3, 23 Yingna Cai/Shutterstock.com; p. 9 Matty Symons/Shutterstock .com; p. 11 Sean Gallup/Getty Images; p. 12 Marco Simoni/robertharding/Getty Images; p. 17 Joe Raedle/Getty Images; p. 18 Carsten Peter/National Geographic/ Getty Images; pp. 20–21 The Washington Post/Getty Images; cover graphics blackpencil/Shutterstock.com.